BREEDERS' E
A KENNEL CLUB

D0567717

Beagle

By Marcia Foy

BREEDERS' BEST ™
A KENNEL CLUB BOOK ®

BEAGLE

ISBN: 1-59378-908-4

Copyright © 2005

Kennel Club Books, LLC
308 Main Street, Allenhurst, NJ 07711 USA
Printed in South Korea

PHOTOS BY:
Paulette Braun,
Isabelle Français,
Karen Ann Taylor,
Justina Fischer,
Carol Ann Johnson and
Bernd Brinkmann

DRAWINGS BY:
Yolyanko el Habanero

Contents

Meet the Beagle

Does the Beagle truly need an introduction? Everyone recognizes this merry little hunting hound with the waggy tail, soft beseeching eyes and the droopy ears. Dog lovers, whether they are weekend sportsmen, field trialers, show aficionados or just dedicated pet owners, can't resist the Beagle for all its down-to-earth charm, effortless charisma and happy-go-lucky attitude toward the world.

Although these small hunting dogs have been around for many a long year, the Beagle's precise origins are something of a shadowy subject. The

He's unmistakable! The Beagle fits the bill of "your best friend" every time, as he's among the most adaptable, affable and affordable dogs in the world.

word "beagle" possibly comes from the Celtic word "*beag*," meaning small; or on the other hand there is (the less likely) chance that it is derived from the French word "*begle*," which has the unfortunate meaning of "useless or of little value." There are various possibilities, not least of which is the connection with the old French "*b'geule*," which could refer to the voice of these hounds, for it meant "gape throat."

"Who are you calling 'useless'?"If this hard-working fellow has anything to say about the etymology of the name Beagle, it's fooey on the French!

Certainly dogs of Beagle-type were known in Greece as far back as 400 BC, and we can trace similar dogs in Britain from AD 200. It is generally believed that the Romans brought small hounds used for rabbit hunting with them to Britain, and that these dogs were bred with local hounds. So there are hounds of varying kinds whose blood runs in the veins of the modern-day Beagle. One of these is the Talbot Hound, a magnificent breed from yesteryear, much larger than the

Here's a pack of very useful hounds, Beagles, that is. In Britain Beagles traditionally were hunted in packs, all following their noses to trail the hare or fox and obeying the signals of the Master of Foxhounds.

Beagle, which was brought to England from France during the Norman Conquest of 1066.

In the 14th and 15th centuries, the Beagle became highly popular with the British monarchs, and when any breed of dog claims fame in royal households, the public takes an interest. "Glove Beagles," as they were called, were tiny enough to fit on a glove, and both Edward II and Henry VII kept packs of these little hounds. Even today the size of Beagles is varied, but better known than the "Glove Beagles" were the "Pocket Beagles," as owned by Britain's Queen Elizabeth I (1533-1603). These were only 9 inches in height when measured to the withers.

But it was not only royalty that owned Beagles in Britain, for many English gentlemen kept private packs. "Pocket Beagles" were carried on horseback in pannier bags and, as their name implies, others were carried in the huntsmen's pockets.

Moving on to the 18th century, there were two main types of hound used for rabbit hunting, the Southern Hound and the North Country Beagle, which was very much faster than the former. However, fox hunting was then becoming increasingly popular, with the result that Foxhounds were on the increase, while Beagles began to fall out of favor. It was fortunate that several farmers in Britain continued to keep Beagles for hunting purposes.

Essentially a small foxhound, the Beagle derives from the larger foxhound breeds such as the English Foxhound, a symmetrical, strong, somewhat stocky scenthound that stands about 27 inches at the withers.

Although we are now only familiar with a short coat on a Beagle, formerly there were both rough- and smooth-coated dogs, similar to the are thought to be the principal ancestors of today's Beagle. These hounds were bred primarily for their hunting ability rather than

Leaner and smaller than his English Foxhound cousin, the American Foxhound stands about 25 inches at the withers and has a long, slightly domed head. The breed goes down in American history as the hound of choice for President George Washington.

coats that can be seen in the scenthounds of France like the Petit Basset Griffon Vendeen and the Basset Fauve de Bretagne.

Interest in the Beagle was rekindled around 1830, and those belonging to a pack owned by Reverend Honeywood in Essex, England

their physical appearance, but later another Englishman, Thomas Johnson, began to combine physical attributes with hunting skills.

The Beagle Club (UK) was formed in 1890, and only a year later came along the Master of the Harriers and Beagles. Both organizations

CHAPTER

1

aimed to further the interests of the breed, albeit each within its own sphere. The first breed show was held in Britain in 1896 and by 1920 much improvement had been made in standardizing type. It is quite amazing that the

English through and through, the Beagle was the choice of aristocrats and commonfolk alike. Today he graces gardens and back yards on both sides of the pond.

annual subscription of one guinea (£1.05) remained thus for no fewer than 80 years, when decimal currency was introduced in Britain.

In the early years of the 20th century, numbers of show Beagles in Britain were few. Only 7 were registered with The Kennel Club in 1927, whereas nowadays there are over 1,000 annual registrations.

And before we leave the Beagle's homeland and move across the Atlantic, readers will be interested to learn that Beagles were even at England's famous educational establishment, Eton. They hunted a drag or an occasional bagged fox, before pursuing the more legitimate sport of fox hunting. The Captain of the Boats was usually the Master, but a kennelman was paid to look after the hounds. The Beagles were not always looked upon favorably by the authorities at Eton, but it was generally thought that they provided excellent training for England's future fox-hunters.

BEAGLES IN THE US

Beagles came to the US in 1876 and were imported from the finest British hunting packs. They not only were used to hunt game for food but also were hunted for sport in braces and in packs. General Richard Rowett of Clairnville was one of the earliest importers of Beagles in the States. His Rowett kennel became known for uniformity of type, show conformation and prowess in the field; the kennel was

Since the American Centennial, the Beagle has been making new friends on US shores. Who could resist this delightful, happy-go-lucky charmer?

CHAPTER

continued by Pottinger Dorsey and Staley Doub. Norman Elmore also played a role in the early years of the breed in the US with his Elmore hounds. Elmore worked together with General Rowett and the Beagles they produced were considered the very best.

The breed was accepted by the American Kennel Club (AKC) in 1884. In 1887 the National Beagle Club of America was formed and soon held its first field trial. This parent club adopted a breed standard that helped the breed to move forward from the "bench-legged" Beagles, meaning they had crooked legs. Such untypical construction had come about as the result of crossing the early English Beagle imports with Dachshunds. At that time in the US there was much controversy regarding the show Beagle versus the Beagle used in field trials. In an endeavor to counter this, from 1896 James Kernochan imported proven hunting hounds from English packs,

Today's Beagle excels in tracking events in which his terrific nose can be put to the test. Few breeds can compete with the nose of a good Beagle.

leading to the breeding of Beagles more akin to those of the present day.

As the 20th century progressed more and more Beagles found themselves in the show rings, with 75 entered at the prestigious Westminster Kennel Club dog show in 1917. At this show they met with significant successes, including first in the Group. Even more fame comes to the breed in field trials, for which there are hundreds of clubs throughout the US, represented in almost all 50 states. There are also a couple of dozen recognized Beagle packs in the US, which goes to show that Americans consider this versatile hunting dog more than just a lovable "Peanut™."

MEET THE BEAGLE

Overview

- Much more than a small hunting dog, today's Beagle is a charis-matic, adaptable companion dog suitable for many different kinds of owners, including sportsmen, show folk, homebodies and trialers.
- The Beagle's origins may date back to pre-Christian Greece and Roman-occupied Britain; in the 14th and 15th century, the breed was popular with British monarchs who favored small examples.
- Later in the 18th century, two types emerged, the North Country Beagle and the Southern Hound; foxhounds and fox hunting outshined the small Beagles, which were mainly kept on farms.
- The Beagles made its way to American shores in the late 19th century, whereupon it became a favorite among hunters, show enthusiasts and pet owners. Today it remains one of the US's most beloved companion dogs.

Are You a Beagle Person?

If you are prepared for your Beagle to look upon you as a human pack member, then you will get along well with each other. If you have a similarly happy, easygoing approach to life, so much the better, for this is a pawn-sized dog with a king-sized zest for life, and he will enjoy your company.

Provided that you have raised your children sensibly, and have taught them to respect animals, your kids will probably be "Beagle people" too. You will have great fun watching

Are you ready to be the leader of the pack? Your Beagle will regard you as his Mistress of Foxhounds, pack leader and best friend in no time flat.

the social interaction between your human family and your canine friend.

You can forget any designs you may have about being a top hair-stylist, for you will not be able to practice on your Beagle, but you will enjoy the necessary short grooming sessions. If you plan to keep your home neat, tidy and clean, you will either need sufficient funds to employ a good cleaning lady, or else you will enjoy using the vacuum, because your Beagle will shed. This is not excessive in comparison with some of the long-coated breeds, and you'll be relieved to know that you will have to do a little less in the way of household chores in the winter months because that is when the coat tends to thicken and shed less. Your expertise with a mop might just come in handy too, for although most Beagles like to be clean, house-training can sometimes be a bit more of a challenge than with other breeds, though not always. If you are

Indoors and out, Beagles make great companions. If you allow your Beagle to sit up on the furniture, be prepared to run the vacuum at least twice a week.

Outdoors Beagles are adaptable and enjoy having a place of their own. For a great doghouse, visit a pet-supply center, build one yourself or call a doggie realtor!

unlucky, you may still be mopping up when your Beagle celebrates his first birthday!

You will also enjoy bathing your Beagle from time to time, especially on those occasions when he has rolled in something particu-larly delightful (to your Beagle, that is; nasty to you!). But that's the fun of owning a Beagle. You'll love it!

Now if you rather fancy being a top-rate dog trainer, again you may just have chosen the wrong breed for Beagles are by no means the

Many Beagle people are lifers and only own Beagles and nothing but Beagles. This happy duo has shared many loving moments throughout their many years together.

easiest dogs to train. But so what if you feel a bit of a fool when attending obedience classes? Some people can certainly manage to train their hounds very success-fully, and you might just be one of those people. (Note, the author said "might.")

A good Beagle owner is a patient one, especially when training the command "Quiet." Have you ever heard a pack of Beagles on the chase, barking and baying and howling? Quite simply, Beagles have been bred to bark when excited. Since you're not offering your Beagle the excitement of a fox chase, your Beagle will bark when a stranger visits your home, when he hears a strange noise, when two leaves fall from the trees instead of one, and so forth. How much patience you need will depend largely on how ready your Beagle is to listen to your commands, how many visitors you have to

your house, how noisy and windy your neighborhood is. Patience will also be one of your virtues when your Beagle decides to chew or destroy something of value, purely because you have not given him enough stimu-lation. Boredom and the Beagle are a very bad combi-nation, so keep your little hound interested, busy and happy.

You needn't be a marathon runner, but you will

Beagle puppies do much more than pose for photographers! Your life with your Beagle pup will involve more than pretty portraits and plastic flowers.

As pack hounds, Beagles are gregarious creatures, thoroughly enjoying the company of other Beagles.

need to be reasonably fit so that you can take your Beagle out on plenty of long walks. But don't be over-enthusiastic while your Beagle is still young, for you should not begin a strenuous running program until your dog is at least a year old. As an apartment dweller, you will simply have to set yourself an exercise schedule with your dog, and you must stick to that as this is a breed that needs not only compan-ionship but physical exercise

too. And that goes for all weather conditions, so be prepared to get on your hiking boots in the winter months and your slicker when it rains. Most Beagles don't mind the rain, snow or humidity.

If you are a handy-man around the house, this will be of great help in cutting down on the sort of bills you would otherwise pay for an odd-job man. Your yard will need to be fully fenced and also "Beagle-proofed." You've gotten yourself an intelligent little dog and if he realizes he can't climb that fence, he may decide to go under it, or even find a way through it. Yes, your toolbox will come in handy.

So, to put it in a nutshell, you have chosen a dog with a fun-loving personality coupled with a bit of stubbornness, lots of voice and a rather independent nature. You will be great as an owner if you are fun-loving

This Beagle puppy has a new friend in his new home, a Sheltie puppy to snuggle with and share fun times.

too, provided you are prepared to train your dog firmly but kindly.

ARE YOU A BEAGLE PERSON?

Overview

- A Beagle person has a zest for life to match his little dog's enthusiasm. He is a patient and kind individual who has the time to train his Beagle, share daily activities and provide a safe, happy home. Beagle folk also own a good vacuum cleaner.
- Somewhat stubborn and always independent, Beagles can be a challenge to train, as they require consistency and structure. Some Beagles can be barky and become bored easily.
- The Beagle person enjoys exercise and is willing to give his dog more than a short walk around the block.
- Beagles offer many rewards to their dedicated owners. They are happy to be in your company and can make any ho-hum day lots of fun.

Description of the Beagle

The Beagle is sturdy, compactly built hound, giving the impression of quality without looking coarse. It should never be forgotten that this is a hound whose primary function is hunting hare, and to do this he follows a scent. The Beagle displays lots of determination and stamina, not to mention his oodles of energy. He is bold, alert and intelligent, and of even temperament.

The American Kennel Club (AKC) recognizes two sizes in the Beagle:

The Beagle's skull should be slightly domed, fairly long and broad, with a square-cut, straight muzzle.

under 13 inches and over 13 to 15 inches, each shown in separate varieties at dog shows. In the UK there is only one height clause, with a minimum height of 13 inches (33 cms) and a maximum height of 16 inches (40 cms). In the US any Beagle measuring more than 15 inches is disqualified. Now that we understand how many inches the Beagle may stand, we encounter an interesting statement at the end of the AKC standard that states that the Beagle is "solid and big for his inches," indicating that he should fill out his height and give the impression of standing tall.

The AKC standard describes the Beagle as "a miniature Foxhound," though his personality makes him appear bigger than life. The inches should either be under 13 or over 13 to 15, denoting separate varieties.

The American standard also differs from the British one in that it actually describes the breed as "a miniature Foxhound," and it gives a compre-hensive scale of points, allocating points for the various head properties, those of the body and those of what is aptly called "running gear."

"Solid and big for his inches," the Beagle gives the impression of standing tall and filling out his inches.

On the American points system, the head of the Beagle scores slightly less than body and running gear, and yet plenty is written about it. The fairly long skull is slightly domed at occiput, with a broad cranium. The medium-length muzzle is straight and square cut, with a well-defined stop, while jaws are level and the lips free from flews. The British standard describes the bite as a "perfect, regular and complete scissor bite, i.e. upper teeth closely overlapping lower teeth and set square to the jaws."

Let's talk ears and neck: the Beagle's ears are low set and long with rounded tips; the Beagle's neck should be strong and slightly arched, free from excess skin.

Because the Beagle hunts by scent, it is to be expected that its ears are low set and long, with rounded tips. It is the length, size and shape of the ears that assist the Beagle on scent hunts, so that they are large and long enough to brush up against the ground and retain the scent. They should extend nearly to the nose when stretched out and hang gracefully, close to the cheeks. The eyes of the Beagle are large, with a mild, appealing expression that is associated with the pleading, gentle hounds.

The throat is free of excess skin, and the strong neck is slightly arched and of sufficient length to allow the hound to reach down easily to scent. The shoulders are muscular and sloping, well laid back and not loaded or heavy so that the animal can move freely and strongly. The forelegs are straight, their bone round and not tapering to the feet. A useful way of assessing the balance of the Beagle is to bear in mind that the height from ground to elbow is roughly half the height at withers. The chest is described as deep and broad, but not too broad; the elbows are firm and the ribs are well sprung, extending well back. This is important for there must be plenty of lung room. Remember this is a compactly built hound, so the couplings are short. Because of the breed's function in life, loins are powerful and supple, but there is no excessive tuck-up, such as one would find in a sighthound like the Whippet.

The Beagle's thighs are muscular for propelling power, the stifles well bent and the hocks firm. When viewed from behind, the legs should be parallel to one another. The feet are tight and firm, well knuckled and strongly padded. A hare foot or an open foot is incorrect. Nails should be kept short.

As the Beagle moves, they should move with a free stride, reaching out well in front and with drive from the rear. He should not roll as a Bulldog does. The sturdy tail is set on high and carried gaily, but should not be curled over the back. It should appear short for the size of

Here's a winning lineup of Beagles at a dog show. Notice the correct front assemblies of the dogs, with straight forelegs and nice tight feet.

the dog and is well covered with hair, called "brush," especially on the underside. The AKC standard faults dogs without brush, referring to such tails as "rat tails."

The Beagle's coat is short, dense and weatherproof. It is close and hard. In fact the AKC standard describes the coat as being of medium length, indicating that it is not short like that of the Smooth

The most recognizable Beagle coloration is the tricolor, a handsome combination of black and tan against a white background.

Dachshund or Miniature Pinscher.

Lastly we come to color, which can be any recognized or "true" hound color; the British standard qualifies that it cannot be liver. This subject has always been one for debate, for it depends how many different breeds of hound are included in this rather nebulous statement. In Europe, there are many unusually colored hound breeds. Certainly the most common color you are likely to come across on a Beagle is the most celebrated of all hound colors, the tricolor, which is a mixture of black, white and tan. Bicolor combinations are also seen in red and white and lemon and white; the black and white combination can also be found but it is very rare.

DESCRIPTION OF THE BEAGLE

Overview

- A member of the scenthound family, the Beagle was created to hunt hare. He is a tireless hunter of great determination and enthusiasm.
- The breed in the US is divided into two varieties: under 13 inches and over 13 to 15 inches; these varieties are shown in separate classes at AKC shows. In the UK, the breed is at least 13 inches and not over 16 inches.
- The head is described as having a fairly long skull that domes slightly at the occiput with a broad cranium; muzzle straight and square; jaws level or scissors bite.
- The Beagle's "running gear" (his legs and feet) allow him to stride freely, reaching out well in front with good drive from the rear.
- The coat is short, dense and weatherproof; the color is any hound color.

Beagle

Skull: Cranium.

Stop: Indentation between the eyes at point of nasal bones and skull.

Muzzle: Foreface or region of head in front of eyes.

Lip: Fleshy portion of upper and lower jaws.

Flews: Hanging part of upper lip.

Withers: Highest part of the back, at the base of neck above the shoulders.

Shoulder: Upper point of forequarters; the region of the two shoulder blades.

Forechest: Sternum.

Chest: Thoracic cavity (enclosed by ribs).

Forequarters: Front assembly from shoulder to feet.

Upper arm: Region between shoulder blade and forearm.

Elbow: Region where forearm and arm meet.

Forearm: Region between arm and wrist.

Carpus: Wrist.

Dewclaw: Extra digit on inside leg; fifth toe.

Occiput: Upper back part of skull; apex.

Topline: Outline from withers to tailset.

Brisket: Lower chest.

Pastern: Region between wrist and toes.

Back: Dorsal surface, extending from the withers.

Loin: Lumbar region between ribs and pelvis.

Body: Region between the fore and hindquarters.

Croup: Pelvic region; rump.

Stern: Tail.

Hip: Joint of pelvis and upper thigh bone.

Hindquarters: Rear assembly from pelvis to feet.

Upper thigh: Region from hip joint to stifle.

Lower thigh: Hindquarter region from stifle to hock; second thigh.

Stifle: Knee.

Flank: Region between last rib and hip.

Hock: Tarsus or heel.

Abdomen: Surface beneath the chest and hindquarters; belly.

Digit: Toe.

Selecting a Breeder

Visiting the breeder's facility will give you a chance to meet the dam and her brood. By the time you meet the puppies, they should be nearly weaned, usually by around the sixth week.

The Beagle is familiar to many people, but the number of breeders is not necessarily high in every part of the world. Americans have long embraced this little hound, and the breed ranks in the top ten in AKC registrations, making a breeder fairly easy to locate. You may be lucky enough to live in an area where there are a few breeders within just miles of your home, but then again you may have to travel some distance. You must also consider whether you want a Beagle as a pet, hunting companion, working dog or show dog. This may make a difference in terms of the breeder you select.

Prospective puppy buyers should always keep foremost in their minds that there are many different kinds of breeder, some with the breed's best interest at heart, others with lesser intentions. It is essential that you locate one who has good dogs you admire, as well as breeding ethics with which you can agree. Sadly, in all breeds, there are invariably some who are simply "in it for the money," and these you must give a wide berth.

Oftentimes the sire will not be on the premises, but on occasion you will be able to meet the dad of the litter, too. His appearance and temperament will indicate much about the likely outcome of the pups.

There are many ways to locate qualified, reliable Beagle breeders. We are living in the "age of information," thanks to the infinite resources of the Internet, printed resources like magazines and newspapers and the hundreds of radio and television stations. Not all sources of information are equal. There are excellent websites and terrible ones. You can

Visiting dog shows makes good sense when you're searching for a Beagle breeder. Many breeders bring five or six dogs to the shows, as well as puppies, and this will afford you a great opportunity to meet the dogs and talk Beagles.

Observe the breeder's rapport with her dogs. If her dogs appear trusting and relaxed in her presence, and obey her readily, you know you have found a reliable source for properly reared dogs.

"Google" Beagle and get over one million references! The website of the National Beagle Club of America and the Beagle Club (UK) are excellent places to start your breeder search.

Another surefire way to find a breeder is to visit a local dog show. There are shows in every region of the country every weekend, and the AKC website (www.akc.org) provides a complete listing of the shows, times and locations. Even though you're not looking for a show puppy necessarily, a dog show is the ideal place to find breeders. Breeder-owners regard the show ring as the testing ground of their breeding programs. This means that they want to prove that their dog or bitch (stud or dam) is worthy of being bred. A dog's championship title essentially tells the public that at least three highly qualified show judges have assessed

Just getting a whiff of a new friend. Don't forget that Beagles are scenthounds and do everything with their noses first.

this dog and evaluated it superior to all of the other Beagles in the show. You can meet many experienced breeders at shows, have the chance to meet their dogs and make the acquaintance of people who "live Beagles." There is no better way to find out if the Beagle breed is for

On the trail of something savory or special, this Beagle keeps his nose low to the ground to keep scent of the quarry.

you than to talk to these Beaglers. Real Beagle people will be happy to advise you, provide recommendations and welcome you into their pack. Beaglers should be as gregarious and friendly as is the hound that they so greatly admire.

Do not open your local newspaper and "order" a puppy from just any person who happens to be selling Beagles (listed in the classifieds between "Batman memorabilia" and "Bugle, used"). You need not be so anxious that you cannot properly research your breeder. Likewise, you should ignore the flyer in the local

delicatessen that says "Pedigree Beegles – Only 5 Left." Approach this acquisition with the same consideration and responsibility that you would the purchase of a car or truck. Your Beagle will likely outlast your Buick that starts to stall out after 10 or 12 years of daily use.

That said, there are many good breeders around, and if you look carefully you will find just such a person. If you can be personally recommended that is perhaps ideal, but you still need to be sure that standards of care are what you expect. You must also be as certain as you can be that the breeder fully understands the breed and has given careful consideration to the way the Beagle has been bred, taking into consideration its pedigree.

The breeder you select may be someone who breeds from home, in which case the puppies will have

The show ring is the proving ground of the whelping box. That means that breeders show their dogs to get the official stamp of approval ("Ch.") from the judges before deciding that the dog is worthy of being bred.

hopefully been brought up in the house and will be familiar with all the activities and noises that surround them. However, the breeder may run a large establishment, so that the litter has perhaps been raised in a kennel situation; though still, if you have chosen wisely, the puppies will have had lots of contact and exposure to various sounds. Beagles thrive in kennel environments so you needn't worry too much if the litter was raised in a kennel. Some of the larger breeding establishments in fact do whelp litters inside the home, and in most instances this is the preferred situation, especially if the

Beagle you are buying is to live in a family environment.

However large or small the breeding establishment, it is important that the conditions in which the puppies are raised are suitable. They should be clean, and the

Meeting the dam of your selected puppy is mandatory. If the dam is not available for you to meet, you will know it's time to keep looking. Look at the sweet, pleading expression on this lovely mom and pup.

puppies should be well supervised in a suitable environment. All should all look in tiptop condition, and temperaments should be sound.

The breeder should be perfectly willing to show you the dam, and it will be interesting for you to take careful note of her own temperament and how she interacts with her offspring. If the dam is not available for you to see, be forewarned that this might be a sign that the puppy was not born on the premises, but has been brought in to be sold. Some breeders work in conjunction with one another, with satellite homes that help raise the puppies away from the main breeder's kennel. If you do your homework, you will know about the breeder and his line before you visit the kennel. What you want to avoid is the breeder who has puppies of multiple breeds for sale and no adult dogs on the premises. Such an establishment is likely just a broker and far from the ideal situation.

As for the stud dog, it is likely that he will not be available, for he may well be owned by someone else, and a careful breeder may have traveled hundreds of miles to use his stud services. Nonetheless, most dedicated breeders will be able to show you a picture of him, or at least provide a pedigree for him.

A well-chosen breeder will be able to give the new puppy owner lots of useful guidance, including advice about feeding. Some breeders give a

When you're visiting the breeder, you may have the advantage of meeting other relatives of the litter, too. It's always nice to meet an aunt or uncle who's a teenager.

small quantity of food to the new owners when the puppy leaves home, but in any event they should always provide written details of exactly what type and quantity of food is fed, and with what regularity. You will of course be able to change this as time goes on, but the change must be gradual.

A breeder will also need to tell you what vaccinations the puppy has received if any, and any relevant documentation should be passed along at the time of purchase. Details about the puppy's worming routine must also be made clear. Many breeders also provide temporary insurance coverage for the puppy. This is an especially good idea, and the new owner can subsequently decide whether or not to continue with this particular policy.

SELECTING A BREEDER

Overview

- Ranking high on the AKC registration list, Beagles number in the thousands and are bred by many breeders. Not every breeder is a breeder worthy of your business.
- Locate a breeder by contacting your national breed club and by visiting dog shows to meet Beagle professionals face to face. Avoid newspaper ads, spurious websites and back-yard hobbyists.
- When you visit the breeder's establishment, you should be impressed by the cleanliness and overall condition of the premises. A breeder whose litter is in his kitchen may be the best of all possible worlds, though larger kennels breed great Beagles, too. Always meet the dam of the litter.
- Trust your chosen breeder for advice about rearing and selecting a puppy.

Finding the Right Puppy

When you go to visit a litter of puppies you are certain to be excited, and the puppies will be excited to see you too. Try not to pick up and cuddle them immediately, but watch how they play with each other and how they react to you. Bear in mind that Beagles often like to play with their mouths; this is not an angry gesture or one of fear, it's simply the way they like to have fun.

A healthy puppy should strike you as being clean, without any sign of discharge from eyes or nose. Its rear end should be spotless, with no indication of loose bowels. Although

The dam may be somewhat protective of her young charges, so make sure she's accepting of you before approaching one of her pups.

any puppy's nails can be sharp, they should not be overly long, indicating that the breeder has clipped them as necessary.

The coat should clearly be soft and resilient, with that unmistakable clean puppy smell. Keep your eye out for any parasites, such as lice, mites or fleas. These tiny bugs cannot always be seen easily, but will be indicated by the puppy's scratching, and you might notice a rash.

Scratching, though, does not always indicate a parasitic or skin condition, for it can also be associated with teething. In this case the puppy will only scratch around his head area, and when the second set of teeth has come through so that the gums are no longer sore, this will stop.

On the other paw, scratching might also be connected with an ear infection, so a quick look inside your new puppy's ears will ensure that there is no build-up of wax, and there

Although temperament is not inherited the same way coloration or eye shape is, for example, it is learned from observation. A friendly dam should rear friendly, outgoing pups.

The puppy you select should be inquisitive and alert to his surroundings. This young Beagle is getting his first smell of the great outdoors.

should be no odor from the ear. Of course, a good breeder will have checked that the puppy is in good health before offering it for sale.

Although by and large Beagles are a fairly healthy lot, the breed as a whole has many hereditary conditions, which mainly affect the eyes,

A sleepy puppy may just be tuckered out. If a puppy remains lethargic throughout the duration of your visit, he may indeed be sick with parasites or an ailment.

hips, elbows, heart, thyroid and eyes. Breeders who belong to the National Beagle Club of America or the Beagle Club in England will be aware of the various screening requirements. In the US, breeders register the results of hip and elbow tests with the Orthopedic Foundation for

Animals (OFA) and eye tests with the Canine Eye Registration Foundation (CERF). Given the long list of conditions from which the Beagle suffers with some frequency, it's important for potential owners to do their best to find Beagles that do not come from unhealthy lines. The money you save on a "bargain puppy" will cost you many times your savings at the vet's office.

Puppy buyers should be aware of the condition known as Beagle dwarfish (sometimes called "funny puppies" or Chinese Beagle syndrome), as well as puppy problems of umbilical hernias, demodicosis (demodetic mange), cleft palates and lips, cryptorchids (undescended testicles) and hermaphroditism. Among the eye problems encountered in Beagles are central progressive retinal atropy (CPRA) and progressive retinal atrophy, glaucoma, keratoconjunctivitis sicca (dry eye), ectopic cilia, distichiasis, imperforate lacrimal punctum and cherry eye. Hip dysplasia, intervertebral disc disease (IDD), brachury (short tail) and luxated patella (slipped knee caps) are among the breed's orthopedic concerns. Hypothryoidism and epilepsy are also seen in great numbers.

Go online to research these conditions. The American parent club can be accessed through the American Kennel Club's website, www.akc.org. Discuss the list of conditions with your breeder. He will not be offended by your questions and should be pleased that you are doing your homework before buying a puppy. Likewise, for the main conditions, the breeder will be able to provide you with written proof of the results, and remember to take note of the dates on which any tests were done.

If you purchase your Beagle from a reputable source, he should live a long, healthy life as your companion and pal.

Although Beagles can sometimes be a little reserved with strangers, they are social animals and temperament is generally friendly. This you should expect in a puppy too, so do not take pity on the overly shy one that hides away in a corner. Your puppy should clearly enjoy your company when you arrive to visit, and this will make for a long-term bond between you. When you go to select your puppy, if possible take with you the members of your immediate family with whom the puppy will spend time at home. It is essential that every member agrees with the important decision you are about to make, for a new puppy will inevitably change all of your lives.

Hopefully you will already have done plenty of research about the breed long before you have reached the stage of having a new puppy enter your lives. Books about the Beagle should be available in quality book stores and pet shops, and as your interest and knowledge in the breed grows, so too should your library. The world of owning Beagles, Beagling and showing Beagles is ever expansive and makes for fascinating reading.

Breed clubs are also an important source of help and information. Some even publish their own leaflets and small booklets about the breed, and might even publish a book of champions,

Adopting two puppies at one time may be more than an inexperienced owner can handle, though some brave owners do just that. Owner, Justina Fisher

so that you can look back to see what your puppy's famous ancestors actually looked like. For aficionados, there are weekly or monthly canine newspapers and magazines, though you may have to subscribe to these as they are not ordinarily available at the news stand, though many large pet shops and book stores may stock them.

Finally, it is a good idea to become a member of at least one breed club. In the US, there are no fewer than two dozen specialty clubs for Beagles, not to mention a couple of hundred field trial clubs dedicated to Beagles. You can access the list of these clubs on the AKC website. By becoming a member of one of these local clubs, you will receive notification of breed club specialty shows, all-breed dog shows as well as field trials. These various events may be interesting to you and provide new opportunities to learn about the Beagle.

FINDING THE RIGHT PUPPY

Overview

- Puppies should be squeaky clean, though they will smell like puppies! A healthy puppy has clear eyes and a clean nose and ears. Keep an eye out for scratching, parasites and loose stools.
- The puppy's coat speaks volumes about the animal's health: it should be soft and resilient with no signs of rash or lice.
- Know about the specific hereditary diseases existent in the Beagle and discuss screening with the breeder.
- Temperamentally Beagles can be slightly aloof, but soon the pups should warm up to your overtures and reveal their naturally gregarious natures.

Welcoming the Beagle Puppy

Because you will want to give your puppy the very best start in life, there are lots of things you will have had to do before the great day of your Beagle's arrival. Be certain that everything at home is as well prepared as it can possibly be.

Unless you are purchasing a puppy from a breeder from another state or province, you should have had an opportunity to meet and select your puppy before the date of arrival. Should this be the case, you will have had plenty of chance to discuss with the breeder exactly what your puppy will need to

Your Beagle will feel safe, comfortable and "at home" in your home if you provide him with a cozy crate to call his own.

make your new Beagle baby's life healthy, safe and enjoyable.

SHOPPING FOR YOUR PUPPY'S THINGS

Depending on where you live, you will probably have easy access to one of the large pet-supply stores or a good privately owned pet shop. Often the latter is owned by people who know dogs well or even operate a grooming shop or training school. Such well-run shops have a wide range of quality items, and the staff will probably be able to give sensible guidance as to what you need to buy. Major dog shows also usually have a wide range of trade stands that cater for every need (and whim), and you are sure to be absolutely spoiled for choice.

For feeding your Beagle, you want bowls that are sturdy, chew-proof and easy to clean.

Meet your most valuable helper in your Beagle's training and safety: his crate. A wire crate is popular for use inside the home, as it gives your curious Beagle an unobstructed view of what's going on around him.

Although owning a dog can be expensive, the outlay of money for

CHAPTER 6

grooming your Beagle puppy will not add up to much. All you need is a soft bristle brush, a slicker brush and a hound glove, all of which are available at the pet shop.

Where your puppy is to sleep will be a major consideration, and you should decide this before the puppy

A nail-clipping device should also be on your shopping list. Keeping the puppy's nails short not only saves you from scratches but also prevents the puppy from tearing his nail on a rug or pavement.

comes home. For Beagle pups, there is only one option for a bedroom: a dog crate. For pet pups, show pups and hunting pups who live inside the

home, the crate offers many advantages, not the least of which are safety and cleanliness. The crate is not only sturdy it's also portable. When your restless newcomer is whining during his first night in your home, you can very easily carry the crate and place it in the corner of your bedroom. The pup will be able to hear you, see you and smell you. Whatever you do, leave him in his crate. Don't let your puppy sleep in your bed. This is a sure way toward owning a spoiled brat of a Beagle who will routinely piddle on your sheets.

You can provide a crate mat or cushion for inside the crate. Make it comfortable, but always select washable bedding. Your puppy will have accidents and it's cheaper to throw the cushion in the washer than in the garbage.

In addition to a crate, you can buy the puppy a nice dog bed for your sitting or TV room. The choice of bedding is very much a matter of personal preference. Bearing in mind that a puppy will not want a bed that is too large, you may have to buy a small sized one to begin with and then a larger one a few months later. Wicker beds may look pretty but they are dangerous, because puppies chew them, and sharp wicker pieces can all too easily injure eyes. It is wiser to choose a durable bed that can be washed or wiped down. This can easily be lined with comfortable soft bedding that can be washed frequently, for it will be important that all your dog's bedding is kept clean and dry. You should also either choose a bed that is just slightly raised from the ground, or else positioned so that it will avoid drafts.

A SAFE HOME

Although the Beagle is relatively small, this is an active breed and can get into

New owners find that their naptimes coincide with their puppies' down time. Puppy ownership is hard work, though it will get easier as your puppy grows up.

all kinds of mischief. Don't forget that this is a scenthound, which means a dog that will sniff and sniff and sniff until he finds something fun to investigate. When Beagle-proofing your home, get down on all fours and think like a hound. The room looks a lot different from this perspective (My, how large are our dust bunnies!). Like your mother always told you, pick up your shoes, socks and yesterday's newspaper. You don't want your Beagle puppy to chew on your good pennyloafers or to piddle on the press!

Everyday household items may seem harmless enough, but draping a dainty cloth over the side of a coffee table full of fragile ornaments is merely tempting fate. Even more dangerous to a mischievous puppy are electric cables, so be sure they are concealed from his reach. Tiny teeth can bite through all too easily, causing what can be a fatal accident. Another word of warning concerns cleaning agents and gardening aids. Many of these contain substances that are

A Beagle pup that receives lots of affection and attention will grow up to be a well-behaved, even-tempered adult dog, one that is a pleasure to have around.

poisonous, so please keep them out of the way of temptation.

SOCIALIZATION
When your puppy first arrives home, it is only natural that you will be proud and will want to show your new-found companion to your friends. However, your puppy is making a big move in his short life, so the first two or three days are best spent quietly at home with you and your immediate family. When your puppy has found his feet and taken stock of his new surroundings, you will be able to introduce him to lots of new people. If you have young children, or if they visit, always carefully supervise any time spent with your young puppy. Youngsters are often attracted by the fun-loving, tail-wagging Beagle, but don't let them assault your dog or toss him about. This Snoopy™ doesn't need to play the Red Baron until he's all grown up!

Just as important as buying the puppy accessories, you must puppy-proof your house. Beagle pups are naturally curious critters that will investigate everything new, then seek-and-destroy just because it's fun. The message here is: never let your puppy roam your house unsupervised. Scout your house for the following hazards:

Trash Cans and Diaper Pails
These are natural puppy magnets (they know where the good smelly stuff is).

Medication Bottles, Cleaning Materials, Roach and Rodent Poisons
Lock these up. You'll be amazed at what a determined puppy can find.

Electrical Cords
Unplug wherever you can and make the others inaccessible. Injuries from chewed electrical cords are extremely common in young dogs.

Dental Floss, Yarn, Needles and Thread, and Other Stringy Stuff
Puppies snuffling about at ground level will find and ingest the tiniest of objects and will end up in surgery. Most vets can tell you stories about the stuff they've surgically removed from puppies' guts.

Toilet Bowl Cleaners
If you have them, throw them out now. All dogs are born with "toilet sonar" and quickly discover that the water there is always cold.

Garage
Beware of antifreeze. It is extremely toxic and even a few drops will kill an adult Beagle, less for a pup. Lock it and all other chemicals well out of reach. Fertilizers can also be toxic to dogs.

Socks and Underwear, Shoes and Slippers, Too
Keep them off the floor and close your closet doors. Puppies love all of the above because they smell like you times 10.

Even though Beagles are generally kind social souls, they still need to have real-life experiences with strangers, children, people in uniform, individuals in wheelchairs and so forth. Dogs that lack socialization are like people

Some Beagles just can't get enough loving!

with no social graces or skills. You want your puppy to fit into our society, just as he fits into his own canine society. Speaking of other dogs, let's talk about introducing your puppy to other dogs.

If your family has other pets, introductions should be made slowly, and under close supervision. Beagles like all other hound dogs get along well with dogs and other animals, but you should always exercise caution until you are certain that all concerned are going to be the best of friends. Even though your affable Beagle baby is happy to meet the neighborhood Rottweiler, perhaps that giant guard dog isn't friendly to other dogs. It's best to know the other dog's temperament before allowing your Beagle to make friends. For the most part, you don't need to interfere, just let canine nature take over and watch your Beagle win over the whole neighborhood.

WELCOMING THE BEAGLE PUPPY

Overview

- Before the puppy comes home, you need to go shopping. Go to a pet shop or pet-supply outlet where you will have a good selection of top-quality merchandise. Your shopping list includes a dog crate, bed, bowls, bristle brush, collar, leash and food.
- Puppy-proof the house and the yard to minimize the mischief. Get on your hands and knees and think like a naughty Beagle. Remove any potentially dangerous items from the puppy's environment.
- Socialization is the key to a well-behaved and well-rounded companion. You want to orchestrate happy social experiences for your Beagle puppy when he gets to meet the family, the neighbor's kids, the dog next door and so on.

Beagle Puppy Kindergarten

When your young Beagle puppy first arrives home, begin by getting him used to the members of your immediate family, allowing him time to take stock of his new surroundings and environment. If you have chosen wisely, you will have a merry little puppy, full of fun and afraid of little. He should be very sociable, but don't overwhelm him with too many visitors and strange faces until he has settled in to your home and knows exactly who his new owners are.

Give your new puppy time to adjust to his new environment, inside and out. Always supervise the puppy whenever he's exploring in the yard.

Depending on the age of your puppy, and whether his course of vaccinations is complete, you may or may not be able to take him out in public places immediately. Whichever the case, I would still advise you to allow him to settle down at home for the first few days, before venturing into the big wide world. There will be lots you can do with your Beagle puppy, so you both undoubtedly will have great fun, but please allow him to get sufficient rest too.

Soft toys that go squeak and squawk will amuse young puppies for hours. Keep your puppy and yourself smiling by choosing safe toys that cannot be destroyed in one play session.

If restricted to your home territory for a little while, you can play games with him, with suitable, safe, soft toys. Check regularly that sharp or unsafe parts, such as squeakers, do not become detached from the toy. These can cause injury, and your puppy's teeth will be very sharp, so toys can easily be damaged.

Whether or not you plan to show your Beagle, it is always good to do a little early training, getting him to

A nice warm bed and a safe chew toy can occupy your Beagle when you're not around to supervise him. Make his home territory fun and safe.

CHAPTER 7

Your young Beagle puppy is a most impression-able creature. Never scold or speak harshly to the puppy. Praise and positive reinforce-ment quickly earn the Beagle's trust.

stand calmly on a table and to lie over to be gently groomed. Both will be helpful on numerous occasions, including visits to the vet when it is much easier to deal with a well-behaved dog, and you will be so proud of your clever companion!

A buckle collar is the best choice for both pup and adult, as it is comfortable for the dog to wear and can be adjusted easily as needed.

Accustom your puppy to being on a lead, which is always a strange experience for a tiny youngster. Begin by just attaching a simple collar, not too tightly, but not so loose that it can be caught on things, causing panic and possible injury. Just put it on for a few minutes at a time, lengthening each period slightly until your puppy feels comfortable in this additional item of clothing. Don't expect miracles—this may take a few days.

Then, when he is comfortable in the collar, attach a small, lightweight lead. The one you select must have a secure catch, yet be simple to attach and release

as necessary. Until now, your puppy has simply gone where he has pleased and will find it very strange to be attached to someone restricting his movements. For this reason, when training my own puppies, I like to allow them to "take" me for the first few

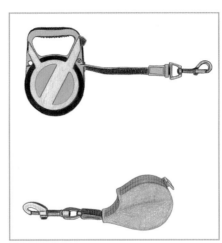

Once your Beagle is accustomed to walking on lead, he can graduate to a retractable lead for your daily walks.

sessions, then I exert a little pressure, and soon enough training can start in earnest, with the puppy coming with me as I lead the way. It is usual to begin training the puppy to walk on your left-hand side. When this has been accomplished to your satisfaction, you can try moving him on your right, but there is absolutely no hurry. If you plan to show your Beagle, you will generally move your dog on your left, but there are occasions when it is necessary also to move him on your right, so as not to obstruct the judge's view.

As your puppy gets older you can teach him to sit, always using the simple one-word command "Sit," while exerting a gentle pressure on his rump, to show him what you expect. This will take a little time, but you will soon succeed, giving plenty of praise when appropriate. Never shout or get angry when your dog does not achieve your aim, for this will do more harm than good. If yours is destined to be a show dog, you may decide not to teach "sit," as in the show ring he will be expected to stand.

When your Beagle puppy can venture into public places, begin by taking him to quiet places without too many distractions. Soon you will find his confidence increasing and you can then introduce him to new places with exciting sights, sounds and smells. He must always be on a thoroughly safe lead that cannot be slipped (quite different from the type of lead that is used in the show ring). When you have total confidence in one another, you will probably be able to let him off the lead, but always keep him in sight, and be sure the place you have chosen for free exercise is safe.

Certainly, in the interest of your Beagle's safety, training and your own sanity, you will need to train your puppy to stay in a crate when required. At most shows, Beagles are housed in crates for at least part of the time while not actually being exhibited in the ring. Crates are also useful for traveling; most dogs seem to look upon them as a safe place to go and don't mind staying in there for short periods, which can be helpful especially for house-training.

When you commence crate training, remain within sight of your dog and give him a toy or something to occupy his mind. To begin with, leave him in the crate for very short spells of just a minute or two, then gradually build up the time span. However, never confine a dog to a crate for more than a few hours at a time. A good rule of thumb is a three-month-old puppy can remain crated for three hours, a four-month-old puppy for four hours and so forth to a maximum of six hours.

Here's the safest place in your whole house: your Beagle puppy's crate! You will soon find that the crate is a multi-purpose device that will make training, travel and safety so much easier.

THE GAME COMMISSION

Puppy games are a great way to entertain your puppy and yourself, while subliminally teaching lessons in the course of having fun. Start with a game plan and a pocketful of tasty dog treats. Keep your games short so you don't push his attention span beyond normal puppy limits.

"Catch me if you can" helps teach the come command. With two people sitting on the floor about 10 or 15 feet apart, one person holds and pets the pup while the other calls him "Snooper, Come!" in a happy voice. Use

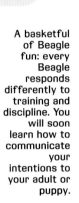

A basketful of Beagle fun: every Beagle responds differently to training and discipline. You will soon learn how to communicate your intentions to your adult or puppy.

the puppy's name to reinforce his recognition. When the pup comes running, give him a giant bear hug and lick of smelly liver. Repeat back and forth several times…don't over do it.

You can add a ball or toy and toss it back and forth for the puppy to retrieve. Even though your Beagle is not a Labrador, he will enjoy a game of fetch. When he picks it up, praise and hug some

more, give him a goodie to release the toy, then toss it back to person number two. Repeat as above.

Another way to teach the come is with good old "hide and seek." Play this game outdoors in your fenced yard or another safe area. When the pup is distracted, hide behind a tree, bush or lawn chair. Peek out to see when he discovers you are gone and comes running back to find you. As soon as he gets close, come out, squat down with arms outstretched and call him "Snooper, come!" You are bonding with your Beagle, using his name and teaching him that he can depend on you to be there.

The "missing-toy caper" is another favorite, since Beagles love to solve problems. Start by placing one of his favorite toys in plain sight and ask your puppy "Where's your toy?" and let him take it. Repeat several times. Then place your puppy safely outside the room and place the toy where only part of it shows. Bring him back and ask the same question. Praise highly when he finds it. Repeat several times. Finally, conceal the toy completely and let your puppy sniff it out with that flawless scenthound nose. Trust his nose…he will find his toy. Games are excellent teaching aids and can be fun for you and your lovable Beagle.

BEAGLE PUPPY KINDERGARTEN

Overview

- During the course of socialization, you can begin your Beagle puppy's first days at school. Dress him for school in his collar and lead and begin acclimating him to walking on his leash.
- A show puppy can be trained to stand on a grooming table. Don't teach the sit exercise until you have mastered the stand/stay.
- Once his inoculations are complete, take him to public places so that he can grow confident.
- Commence crate training so that your puppy accepts the crate as his bedroom and den.
- Games are fun and lay the foundation for responding to his name and important commands.

House-training Your Beagle

A puppy piddling in the grass—a sight that makes every new owner breathe easy to know he has gotten the pup there in time!

Let's dispel the myth that Beagles are impossible to house-train. Beagles are no more difficult to house-train than other dogs, provided the owners are consistent and dedicated to their training. Your breeder will tell you that it is imperative that you are consistent, day in and day out, until your Beagle puppy is reliably housebroken.

If you keep your Beagle in the home, once house-trained you should not have any particular doggy odor around, provided you groom your dog regularly. To house-train with success, you will need to be firm, but never harsh, and you must certainly never be rough with your Beagle.

When your puppy first arrives in your home, he may or may not already be house-trained, albeit to a limited extent. Many breeders begin the house-training effort before the puppies leave for their new homes. However, you must always realize that your home is completely different from the last, so he will have to re-learn the house rules. Doors will not be located in the same places, your family may go to bed and rise at different times, and it will undoubtedly take him a little time to learn and to adapt.

Above all be consistent in your house-training routine. You must be vigilant full-time when setting out to house-train your Beagle.

The speed of your house-training success will depend to a certain extent on your own environment, and to the season of the year. Most puppies are perfectly happy to go out into the yard in dry weather, but when it is pouring, many feel rather

More so than most other dogs, Beagles are professional sniffers, aka scenthounds. Sometimes their noses get in the way of their brains, ears and bladders.

CHAPTER 8

differently and will need some encouragement. Fortunately, most Beagles don't mind getting their paws wet and will go out in most weather.

Most agree that the best way to house-train a Beagle

An adult or puppy Beagle never wants to soil his sleeping quarters and therefore will hold his bladder until he's released. Of course, adults can hold their water for longer periods than a puppy can.

can be summed up in one simple word: crate. It's your puppy's most critical accessory. Purchase a medium-sized wire or fiberglass crate from the pet store

and it will last your dog's lifetime. Dogs by nature do not like to sleep out in the open. You will rarely find your puppy sleeping in the middle of the patio or living room floor. More likely he will choose a place that is secluded and hidden from potential predators, such as under a table, in a corner or behind a sofa. The crate provides a den-like environment, which the dog would welcome in the wild.

The dog's natural instinct is to keep his den clean, thus he will not urinate or defecate in his sleeping area. Crate training is based on this simple principle, and Beagle owners must commit themselves to establishing a routine with their dogs. Put the puppy in the crate whenever you cannot keep an eye on him in the house.

Let him nap during the day in his crate, setting aside certain times each day that you will call "crate time." When your Beagle hears you announce "Crate time!" (in a happy voice), he will know the day, you can leave the crate door open so that your puppy can come and go as he pleases. You'll see that the puppy will opt to spend time in his crate on his own. The crate is a great escape from

Pre-pee: that is asleep. The first thing a puppy does when he wakes up from a nap is piddle. That makes him no different than his owner, come to think of it.

it's time to go to his den. At night the Beagle will sleep in his crate.

Each time you release the puppy from his crate, you must lead him outside to do his business. Do not open the crate and ignore the puppy. You must take him outside right then and there. During the busy house, a fun place to chew on a favorite toy and a cool doggy hangout.

Another option for house-training the puppy, though not a permanent solution, is paper training. Many owners find this useful in the very early stages of training. Folded newspaper (a thickness of five or six sheets) should be placed by the door, so that the dog learns to associate the paper with the exit to the wide world outside, and when he uses the paper he should be praised. Obviously it is ideal if the puppy can be let out as soon

Imagine what the grass smells like to a scenthound. Your Beagle puppy will quickly learn that the grass is the place to do his business, as it smells and feels better than your antiseptic flooring.

as he shows any sign of wanting to do his business, but again this may depend upon whether your home has immediate access to an outdoor area.

Remember that puppies need to go out much more frequently than adult animals, certainly immediately after waking, being let out of their

crates and following a meal. In fact to take them outside every hour while they are awake is not a bad idea at all. Always keep both your eyes and ears open, for a youngster will not be able to wait those extra two or three minutes until it is convenient for you to let him out. If you delay, accidents will certainly happen, so be warned.

As your puppy matures, signaling to be let out when necessary will become second nature, and it is rare to encounter an adult Beagle that is unclean in the house. A stud dog, however, can be different, for he may well want to mark his territory, and your table and chair legs may be just the places he decides to mark.

A simple one-word relief command can be very helpful: "potty," "outside" or "toilet" seems to work well. Never, ever forget to give praise when the deed is done in the desired place. However, if an accident happens, you should indeed give a verbal reprimand, but this will only work if your Beagle is caught *in the act*. If you try to reprimand him after the event, he simply will not know what he has done wrong, and this will only serve to confuse him.

It is essential that any mess is cleaned up immediately and thoroughly with an odor-remover. If a dog has done his toilet in the wrong place, this must be cleaned thoroughly so as to disguise the smell, or he will smell his urine and want to use that particular place again. When your puppy is old enough to be exercised in public places, carry with you a "pooper-scooper" or small plastic bag, so that any mess can be removed. The anti-dog lobby exists in every country, so please give them no cause for complaint.

HOUSE-TRAINING YOUR BEAGLE

Overview

- Beagles can be house-trained just as can any other dog. They require consistency on their owners' parts because hounds aren't the tidiest of canines and Beagles are a wee bit stubborn.
- House-training also can be spelled C R A T E. Beagles respond to crate-training naturally, accepting the crate as their dens, which they instinctively want to keep clean.
- Teach a command to encourage your Beagle to enter his crate. Let him spend time in the crate, including his nighttime sleep.
- Paper training is a temporary method of teaching the dog clean habits; it also can be used in conjunction with crate training.
- Institute a relief command so that your puppy knows that you want him to do his business whenever you say the "potty" word.

Teaching Basic Commands

Because Beagles are intelligent dogs that like to solve their own problems, this can make them something of a challenge when it comes to training. But no two dogs are alike, and you will basically have to find a training method that suits your own dog. Always keep in the back of your mind that Beagles can get bored rather quickly, at which time they will decide to look for a bit of fun. Some show dogs are obedience trained too, but many exhibitors feel this can be detrimental to a dog's performance in the

Portrait of a problem-solver: the Beagle loves to think for himself and often finds the ideas of humans inferior to his own.

show ring. If you plan to show your Beagle, you will have to bear this in mind from the outset.

In all training, it is essential to get your dog's full attention, which many owners do with the aid of treats, so that the dog learns to associate treats with praise. Many Beagles respond well to treats, but not all owners like to use them. As long as treats are used wisely and in moderation, they are the perfect motivators for the ever-famished Beagle.

The following training method involves using food treats, although it should be possible to wean your dog off these training aids in time. Always use very simple commands, just one or two short words, and keep sessions short, so they do not become boring for your dog.

SIT

With the lead in your left hand, hold a small treat in your right, letting

Since the sit position is the starting point of many other commands, trainers commonly begin with teaching the sit exercise first.

The training halter proves an excellent option for obedience lessons with the Beagle, as it provides better control of the dog.

Show dogs master the art of heeling on lead as they show off their confident and free gait.

your dog smell or lick the treat, but not take it. Move it away as you say "Sit," your hand rising slowly over the dog's head so that he looks upward. As your Beagle looks upward, he should automatically sit. If this simple method doesn't work, put a little pressure on your dog's hindquarters to give him the idea of what you want.

HEEL

A dog trained to walk to heel will walk alongside his handler without pulling. Again the lead should be held in your left hand, while the dog assumes the sit position next to your left leg. Hold the end of the lead in your right hand and control it lower down with your left.

Step forward with your right foot, saying the word "heel." To begin with, just take three steps, then command him to sit again. Repeat this procedure until he carries out the task without pulling. Then you can increase the number of strides, five, seven and so on. Give verbal praise at the close of each section of the exercise. At the end of the training session, let him enjoy himself with a free run.

DOWN

When your dog is proficient in sitting, you can introduce the "down." Firstly it is essential to understand that a dog will consider the down position as a submissive one, so gentle training is important.

With your Beagle sitting by your left leg, as for the "sit," hold the lead in your left hand and a treat in your right. Place your left hand on top of the dog's shoulders (without pushing) and hold the treat under his nose, saying "Down," in a quiet tone of voice. Gradually move the treat along the floor, in front of the dog, all

Use a treat to teach your Beagle the down position. A little smelly liver can make any exercise more enjoyable.

the while talking gently. He will follow this, lowering himself down. When his elbows touch the floor, you can release the treat and give praise, but try to get him to remain there for a few seconds before getting up. Gradually the time of the down exercise can be increased.

STAY

Stay can be taught with your dog either in a sit or in a down position, as usual with

Reinforce the stay command with a hand signal. Beagles like the stay command, which essentially translates to "do nothing until you hear from me."

the lead in your left hand and the treat in your right. Allow him to lick the treat as you say "Stay," while standing directly in front of the dog, having moved from your position beside him. Silently count to five, then move back to your original position alongside, allowing your dog to have the treat, while giving him lavish praise.

Keep practicing the "stay" as described above for a few days, then gradually increase the distance between you, using your hand with the palm facing the dog, indicating that he must stay. Soon you should be able to do this exercise without a lead, and your Beagle will increasingly stay for longer periods of time. Always give lavish praise upon completion of the exercise.

COME

Your Beagle will love to come back to you when called. The

idea is to invite him to return, offering a treat and giving lots of praise when he does so. It is important to teach the come command, for this should bring your dog running back to you if ever he is danger of moving out of sight.

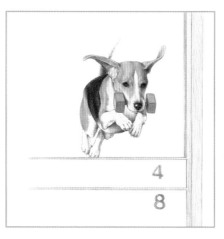

A joyous sight: a Beagle in flight over the high jump at an obedience trial. Once your Beagle has mastered the sits and downs, he can reach new heights in competitive events.

TRICKS

The Beagle is a happy character that can be full of fun; he might just enjoy learning the odd trick or two. What you teach, if anything at all, will be very much a matter of choice, but always remember that a Beagle is a hound first and foremost.

TEACHING BASIC COMMANDS

Overview

- Big-Beagle school starts now: teaching the commands. Keep it fun, brief and positive. Beagles bore easily because they are bright, eager hounds.
- A little liver goes a long way...use treats to reward your Beagle for properly executed commands.
- Sit, heel, down, come and stay make up the Beagle's repertory of basic commands.
- Practice a command a few times a day. Don't proceed to the next lesson until the dog has mastered the previous command.
- Beagles don't sell many tickets at the circus—don't expect your Beagle to jump through hoops, but you can rely on him to do the basics and maybe a few cute party tricks.

Feeding Your Beagle

P rovided that a high-quality diet is given, the amount of food needed by a Beagle is surprisingly small for such an active hound. Most Beagles are good eaters, sometimes referred to as "good doers," so as a responsible owner you will need to monitor his weight carefully. Beagles, as a rule, are chow hounds—they love their food and never know when they're full. You don't want your Beagle's bottomless stomach to lead to obesity, so you must be your Beagle's dietician as well as his caregiver.

When it's time to eat, your Beagle will let you know it. Don't go by him though, as Beagles are always hungry.

Today there is an enormous range of specially prepared foods available for dogs, many of them scientifically balanced and suitable for all age ranges. It is really a matter of personal preference as to which particular food you decide to feed, though initially this will undoubtedly be influenced by the make and type of food that has been fed to your new puppy by his breeder. Changes can of course be made to this, but never change suddenly from one food to another, or your Beagle is likely to get an upset tummy. Introduce a new brand of food gradually over a few days, until the old brand is phased out. There is usually no harm at all in changing the flavor of the food, while keeping with the same brand. This can add some variety to the diet, or you might prefer to add a little flavored stock to tempt the palate.

Select a high-quality puppy food for your Beagle pup and don't be tempted to supplement his diet with table scraps or special treats.

Different dogs have different needs. By working closely with your veterinarian and your breeder, you will be able to devise a feeding regimen that will keep your Beagle fit and trim.

Should you decide to feed a dry product, make sure you thoroughly read the feeding instructions, for some need to be soaked, especially those for youngsters. Dry food should also be stored carefully, bearing in mind that its vitamin value declines if not used fairly quickly, usually within about three months. It is essential that a plentiful supply of fresh water is available for your dog when feeding dry foods in particular, though adult dogs should have access to water at all times.

Because of the enormous range of products available,

Senior dogs require less calories per day than do their adult counterparts. As the Beagle's metabolism slows, a senior or light diet will help keep your old-timer in shape.

Monitor your Beagle's weight so that you know when you're feeding too much or too little. You want to be able to detect a waistline below the rib cage. Don't let those soft, pleading eyes convince you to add any gravy to his kibble.

you may find it difficult to decide which to choose without advice from another Beagle enthusiast. However, keep in mind that in adulthood, an active dog will always require a higher protein content than one that lives a sedentary life. No dog should be fed chocolate, as this is carcinogenic to dogs. Additionally, many human

Your Beagle's coat and general condition rely upon your selection of a high-quality adult dog food. Find out which brand your breeder uses and start with that one. Once you find a food your Beagle likes (not hard to do!), you should stick with it.

foods (like grapes, onions, nuts and the pits of certain fruits) are harmful to dogs. Some owners prefer to feed fresh foods, but this being the case they should be absolutely certain that they are feeding a well-balanced diet, and that no dangerous things like cooked chicken bones are included in the meals.

Many owners are tempted to feed tidbits between meals, but this is not a good idea as the weight can pile on almost imperceptibly. A very suitable alternative is to give the occasional carrot.

Providing safe chew toys for your Beagle can help to ensure that he has strong teeth that will last a lifetime.

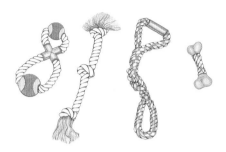

Most dogs love them! Carrots don't put on any weight and are a useful aid to keeping the teeth clean.

How many times a day you feed your adult Beagle will probably be a matter of preference. Many people feed a small amount morning and evening, others prefer to give just one meal, perhaps with a light snack at the other end of the day. Puppies need to be fed as many as four times daily; your own dog's breeder will hopefully have given you good advice in this

Active dogs require more calories than sedentary dogs. If your Beagle is running and playing all day, he will need more food than if he's simply posing for his sculpture all day.

regard, and the transition to one or two meals a day will be made gradually.

As a dog gets older his metabolism changes, so feeding requirements may change, typically from one large meal a day to two or even three smaller ones. By then of course you will know your pet well and should be able to adjust feeding accordingly, but if you have any queries your vet will almost certainly be able to guide you in the right direction.

Once your Beagle reaches the age of around eight or nine months, you'll want to switch to an adult formula. Feeding the adult twice a day is preferable to a single daily meal.

FEEDING YOUR BEAGLE

Overview

- You've just read your Beagle's favorite chapter in this book: the one about food, glorious food! Beagles are uncommonly good eaters—they are hungry unless they're eating.
- Monitor your Beagle's weight and waist. Don't let his pleading eyes, supersonic nose and bottomless stomach lead to obesity. Don't add extras to his bowl and limit treats for when he's being trained.
- Discuss the brand and type of food with your breeder. His experience with feeding dogs of his line is invaluable in making this decision. If you decide to change brands, do so gradually.
- Adult dogs should be fed twice per day; puppies should eat three or four times, depending on their age and activity level. Active Beagles require more food than sedentary dogs.

Home Care for Your Beagle

B ecause you think the world of your Beagle, you will want to do all within your power to keep him in the best of health. To do this, routine care on a daily basis will be important. This will help you to see problems arising, so that you can take your pet to the vet without delay for further investigation.

Yes, you have to brush your Beagle's teeth. A twice weekly toothbrushing will keep your Beagle's teeth white and his breath fresh-smelling.

DENTAL CARE

Keeping teeth in good condition is your responsibility, and you owe this to your dog for dental problems do not just stop inside the mouth. When gums are infected, all sorts of health problems subsequently can arise, spreading through the system and possibly leading even to consequent death.

Clean your Beagle's teeth using a toothbrush and special canine tooth-paste. Your dog may not like this procedure at first, but he should easily get used to it if you clean regularly. Experienced breeders sometimes use a special dental scraper, but damage can be done with this, so I do not recommend it for use by the average pet owner.

When cleaning the teeth, always check the gums for signs of inflam-mation. If you notice that the gums look red or swollen, a visit to your vet would be worthwhile. Dental clean-liness can be aided by your dog chewing suitable chews, safe cooked bones or even carrots.

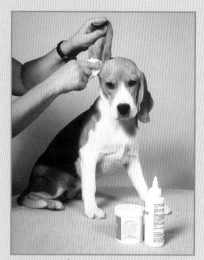

Your Beagle's large floppy ears don't allow much air to flow into his ear canal, thus making him prone to ear infections. Clean out your Beagle's ears on a weekly basis.

Provide hard chew toys for your Beagle to use to clean his teeth and gums between brushings. He doesn't know he's cleaning his teeth, so don't tell him.

A healthy, happy Beagle looks well kept and shares his life with responsible, caring owners. Your Beagle should look as resilient and lovely as this handsome youngster.

CHAPTER 11

FIRST AID

Accidents can happen, and if they do you must remain as cool, calm and collected as possible under the circumstances. For example, insect stings are quite frequent and, if it's still there, the sting should be removed with tweezers. Ice can be applied to reduce the swelling and accurate dosage of antihistamine treatment given. If a sting is inside the mouth, consult your vet at once.

Accidental poisoning is also a worry, as dogs can investigate all sorts of things, not all of which are safe. If you suspect poisoning, try to ascertain the cause, because treatment may vary according to the type of poison taken. Vomiting or sudden bleeding, such as from the gums, can be indications of poisoning. Urgent veterinary attention is essential.

Small abrasions should be cleaned thoroughly and antiseptic applied, but in the case of serious bleeding, initially apply pressure above the area. For minor burns, apply cool water.

In the case of shock, such as following a car accident, keep the dog warm while veterinary aid is sought without delay.

For heat stroke, cold water must be applied immediately, especially over the shoulders, but in severe cases if possible the dog should be submerged in water up to his neck. Dogs can die quickly from heat stroke, so urgent veterinary attention is of paramount importance. Conversely, in the case of hypothermia, keep the dog warm with hot-water bottles and give a warm bath if possible.

RECOGNIZING SIGNS OF GOOD HEALTH

If you love your Beagle and you spend plenty of time together, you will know when something is amiss. He may go off his food or seem dull and listless. His eyes, usually bright and alive, may seem to have lost their sparkle, and his coat may look more dull than usual.

His relief habits may also be an indication if ill health. Loose bowels usually clear up within 24 hours, but if they go on for longer than this, especially if you see blood, you will need to visit your vet. Also keep a look out for increased thirst and an increase in frequency of urination, which could indicate a problem.

CHECKING FOR PARASITES

It is essential to keep your dog's coat in excellent condition, or parasites may take a hold and the skin condition deteriorates. It is often not easy to see parasites, and if you catch sight of even one flea you can be sure there will be more lurking somewhere. There are now

Beagle housemates play together, sleep together and sometimes groom each other. When it comes to Beagles, two is definitely better than one.

several good preventive aids available for external parasites, and your vet will be able to advise you about these, for sometimes the best remedies are not available in shops.

Also be on the look out for signs of ear mites. A brown discharge with some odor in the ear is a clear indication that they are present. A suitable ear treatment will be available from your vet.

A dog can also carry internal parasites in the form of worms. Roundworms (ascarids) are the most common, and tapeworms, although less frequent, can be even more debilitating.

Heartworms are transmitted by mosquitoes and can cause a very serious disease in dogs. Discuss preventives with your vet. These oral medicine can be taken monthly or even less frequently, depending on where you live. Routine worming is essential throughout a dog's life and, again, veterinary recommendation as to a suitable regimen is certainly advised.

HOME CARE FOR YOUR BEAGLE

Overview

- As your Beagle's keeper, you are responsible for his maintenance and overall health.
- Keep your Beagle's smile white and his breath clean-smelling. Brush the dog's teeth regularly and check his gums for inflammation.
- Don't wait for an emergency to educate yourself in first aid. Equip yourself with the necessary accessories and knowledge.
- Be observant of your dog's condition and behavior so that you know when he's "off."
- You are the bug patrol. Check your Beagle's coat for parasites, bites and droppings. Make sure his stools look normal every day.

Grooming Your Beagle

Y our Beagle has a short coat that must never be neglected if you wish to keep your dog in good condition and health. Just think of a human with short hair, it must still be kept clean and combed, or it would feel most uncomfortable. Ideally your Beagle will be groomed on a sturdy table, with a non-slip surface. You will find that owners use slightly different pieces of equipment, according to what they find suits best. When buying your new puppy, you should receive good advice from the

Basically a clean fellow, even the Beagle needs a bath now and then. A bucket of sudsy fun and lots of towels and you're on your way to a squeaky clean Beagle.

breeder about grooming and equipment, but doubtless you will develop your own preferences over time. The most popular items of equipment for this breed are a natural bristle brush, a slicker brush and a hound glove, but you may also like to have a metal comb.

A hound glove makes an ideal grooming tool for the Beagle's short, sleek coat. You'd be surprised how many little hairs your Beagle drops on a daily basis.

COAT CARE

How frequently you choose to bathe your Beagle will depend to a large extent on your dog's lifestyle, but it is essential to keep the coat clean and to groom regularly. A quick once-over every day is always a good idea. This will only take you a few minutes, but this way you can keep the coat healthy and shiny.

In a full grooming session, some people like to comb through the coat first with a metal comb. This will help to remove any dead hair and in doing this you will see if any dirt has built up in the coat, which will probably

Your Beagle's grooming tools should include a slicker brush, comb and bristle or pin brush. His coat will look its shiny best with a daily once-over.

mean that you will decide to bathe your Beagle. On the other hand, several owners who groom regularly manage without a comb at all, just using a brush.

Even if you have combed through, you will still need to use a brush to go through the coat again. After this you should use the hound glove, which will both groom the coat and massage the skin. Surely your Beagle will enjoy a good massage!

Entowel your Beagle with soft terry and lots of love. Make sure your Beagle is completely dry before letting him out in cold weather.

BATHING YOUR BEAGLE

Imagine if we had to bathe our dogs every day as we do ourselves? Fortunately, dogs do not require frequent bathing, though an occasional bath helps ensure that your Beagle's coat remain clean and resilient and his skin pliant and healthy. If you exhibit your Beagle, you will probably wish to bathe more frequently than someone who owns a pet or a working dog. If a puppy is accustomed to being bathed from a young age, he will be perfectly happy to accept this part of the grooming procedure as he grows older. It's not uncommon for show exhibitors to bathe their dogs before every show, which could mean weekly.

Always brush your Beagle's coat thoroughly before bathing, then stand your dog on a non-slip surface, and test the water temperature on the back of your own hand. Use a doggy shampoo, not a human one, taking care not to get water into the eyes and ears. It is usually wise to wash the head last, so that shampoo does not drip into the eyes while you are concentrating on another part of the body. Take care to reach all the slightly awkward places, so that no area is neglected. It is essential that all soap is thoroughly rinsed out so that no residue remains in the coat.

Having carefully lifted your Beagle out of the bathtub wrapped in a warm, clean towel, dry him with the aid of an electric blow dryer set on low. Be aware that he can catch cold when wet. Remember that many dogs do not like air blowing toward their faces so be considerate and aware of this when drying your Beagle.

EARS AND EYES

It is important to keep your Beagle's eyes and ears clean. They should be carefully

wiped, perhaps using one of the proprietary cleaners available from good pet stores. Because the Beagle has long floppy ears, these should always be checked regularly as they can be more prone to a waxy build-up than a smaller ear that stands upright.

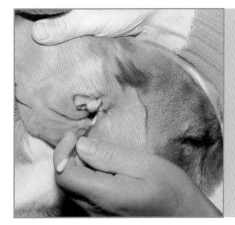

The Beagle's long floppy ears require weekly cleaning with a good ear-cleansing solution. Check them regularly for signs of mites, wax accumulation and dirt.

If your dog has been shaking his head or scratching at his ears, there may well be an infection or ear mites. A thick brown discharge and malodorous smell are also indicative of these problems, so veterinary consultation is needed right away.

CHAPTER 12

At any sign of injury to the eye, or if the eye turns blue, veterinary attention must be sought immediately. If an eye injury is dealt with quickly, it can often be repaired, but if neglected this can lead to loss of sight.

An electric or battery-operated nail grinder with a sandpaper head is an ideal tool for keeping your Beagle's nails short and polished.

NAILS AND FEET

Nails must always be kept trimmed, but how frequently they need clipping depends very much on the surface upon which your dog walks. Those living their lives primarily on carpets or on grass will need more frequent attention to their nails than those who regularly walk on a hard surface.

Your Beagle should be trained to accept nail clipping from an early age. Take great care not to cut into the quick, which is the blood vessel that runs through the nail, for this is painful. It is a good idea to keep a styptic pencil or some styptic powder on hand in case of an accident. Cutting just a small slither of nail at a time is the safest approach.

Another option for nail care is the grinder, which many groomers find preferable. If you opt for the grinder, you should accustom the puppy first to the sound of the mechanism's motor. Some Beagles dislike the noise more than the sensation the grinder causes. You can turn the grinder on and let it run on top of the counter while you play with your dog or brush him. When it's time to introduce your Beagle to the grinder, he will not be afraid of the noise. The advantage of using the grinder is that you can't cut into the quick, and if you do, the heat will instant cauterize the bleeding. Nail grinders are sold in most good pet shops.

You should also inspect feet regularly to be sure that the pads have not become cracked and that nothing has become wedged or embedded between them. Even road tar can get stuck on the pads, and butter is useful for removing this should it happen.

ANAL GLANDS

A dog's anal glands are located on either side of the anal opening. Sometimes these become blocked and require evacuation. Experienced breeders often do this themselves, but pet owners would be well advised to leave this to their vet, for damage can be caused and evacuation is not always necessary and never pleasant.

GROOMING YOUR BEAGLE

Overview

- Even though your Beagle doesn't have the high-maintenance coat of a Poodle or Chow Chow, you still have to own a brush. We recommend a slicker brush, bristle brush and a hound glove, and maybe a metal comb.
- Brush your Beagle every day, just to keep his coat shiny and clean. It will take no more than a minute or two.
- Acclimate the puppy to the bath early on. Although most Beagles don't mind the water, it's helpful to have a cooperative dog when bathing. Once a month suffices for most owners.
- Keep your Beagle's eyes and ears clean and free of debris. Floppy ears can be prone to wax build-up.
- Keep your Beagle's nails short by clipping them or using the grinder. Don't forget to check his anal glands.

Keeping Your Beagle Active

Here's a superhero Beagle flying over the jump at an agility trial! With training and lots of praise, your Beagle can reach any heights.

Beagles are very adaptable dogs and lead a variety of lifestyles, so how much exercise they need will depend very much on how they have been brought up. A dog used in the field will of course be used to traveling miles on foot, but a pet or show Beagle is usually content with substantially less.

Nonetheless, every dog loves to investigate new places and new smells, and the Beagle is no exception. Regular exercise not only will help to keep him fit but also will serve to keep his senses alert. Although reasonably small, your Beagle should be kept in the peak of physical condition. Bearing in mind that Beagles seem prone to putting on excess weight, too sedentary a lifestyle is not recommended.

When fully trained, some Beagles are fairly obedient off lead, but remember that the Beagle is a scenthound and has a great hunting instinct and may just decide to go where his fancy (or nose) takes him. His nostrils may detect an interesting smell on the other side of the fence or up the street. It is also important that your Beagle is not left damp, following exercise in inclement weather.

Some affable Beagles are now used in therapy work, visiting nursing homes and hospitals to meet people less fortunate than their owners. The breed's convenient size makes the visit something to which patients

Look how easily this Beagle is clearing the wall at an agility trial! The Beagle's wondrous ears act as power sails to lift him high off the ground...or he's just a really great jumper.

Beagles hunt in packs. If you're interested in seeing your Beagle running with other Beagles, look into breed clubs in your area.

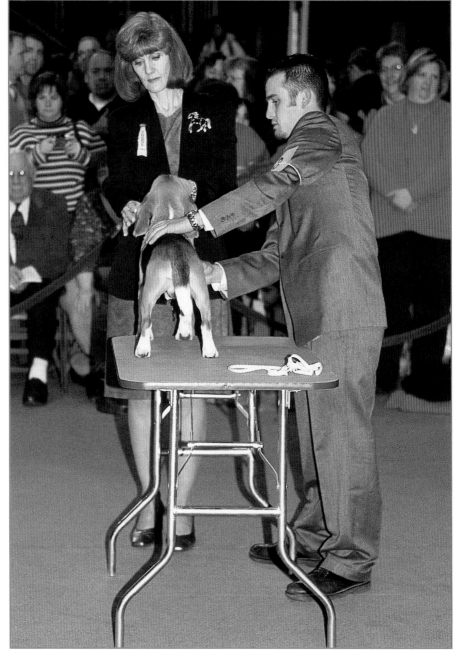

Any registered Beagle can enter a dog show, provided that he's not neutered or spayed and doesn't have any disqualifying faults.

and the elderly greatly look forward. It is also not unknown for a Beagle to become a "hearing dog." This is a dog that is especially trained to listen for sounds like telephones and doorbells ringing, something of great assistance to an owner with impaired hearing.

Well-trained Beagles, owned by smart and patient owners, take part in obedience trials held in conjunction with AKC conformation shows. More commonly, Beagles participate in field trials that are run by the AKC or individual breed clubs. There are three types of trials available to Beagles: the Brace (for two or three hounds together); Small Pack (for groups of seven hounds); and Large Pack (for large groups of uncounted hounds). The dogs are judged on their skill, accuracy and speed with which they trail and find rabbits and hares, the traditional quarry of the eagle-nosed Beagle. The Beagle trials are the only AKC event designed for a single breed of dog. Doesn't that show you how smart and unique the Beagle truly is?

KEEPING YOUR BEAGLE ACTIVE

Overview

- Hunting and field dogs will require more activity than show dogs and pets. Base your Beagle's exercise regimen on his job description.
- Few breeds are as adaptable as Beagles. They can adjust to a very active lifestyle or a fairly sedentary one.
- Well-socialized Beagles make excellent therapy dogs; some breed representatives are employed as "hearing dogs" for the deaf.
- Beagles excel in field trials and can participate in braces or packs. Find out about Beagle field-trial clubs in your area.

BEAGLE

Your Beagle and His Vet

Some dogs seem not to mind going to the vet at all; others simply hate it and know exactly where they are as soon as they get out of the car. However, the Beagle is a friendly little fellow, so try to make his veterinary visits as pleasurable as possible. If you personally are nervous about the visit, this will almost certainly be transmitted to your dog.

It is sensible to make early contact with your vet, in part to

Discuss your Beagle puppy's inoculation schedule with your veterinarian. He needs to have his complete vaccinations before you can begin taking him outside your home and yard.

build up rapport for any consequent visits. Obviously if your puppy's course of vaccinations is not yet complete, you will need to take him to the vet in any case, but it is a good idea to take him along for a health check-up anyway.

Only allow your puppy to spend time with other puppies that you know, so that you can be sure that your puppy is not exposed to infectious diseases.

If you do not already have a vet for other family pets, you should select carefully. Preferably take recommendation from someone who has dogs of his own and whose opinion you trust. Location is also an important factor, for you must be able to get your dog there quickly in an emergency and the vet must be able to respond rapidly when needed. If you live in a rural area, please be sure that you choose a vet who has plenty of dealings with small animals. Many have a great deal of experience with farm animals, but sadly their experience with dogs is limited, something I have learned firsthand in the past.

Select a veterinarian who knows and likes Beagles. Your dog's continued health relies on your vet's care and knowledge.

VACCINATIONS

The vaccines recommended by the American Veterinary Medical Association are called CORE vaccines, those which protect against diseases most dangerous to your puppy and adult dog. These include: distemper (canine distemper virus – CDV), fatal in puppies; canine parvovirus (CPV or parvo), highly contagious and also fatal in puppies and at-risk dogs; canine adenovirus (CAV2), highly contagious and high risk for pups under 16 weeks of age; canine hepatitis (CA1) highly contagious, pups at high risk. These are generally combined into what is often called a 5-way shot. Rabies immunization is required in all 50 states, with the vaccine given three weeks after the complete series of the puppy shots.

Non-CORE vaccines, no longer routinely recommended by the AVMA except when the risk is present, are canine parainfluenza, leptospirosis, coronavirus, Bordetella (kennel cough) and Lyme disease (Borreliosis). Your veterinarian will alert you if there is an incident of these non-fatal diseases in your town or neighborhood so you can immunize accordingly.

The American Animal Hospital Association (AAHA) guidelines recommend vaccinating adult dogs every three years instead of annually. Research suggests that annual vaccinations may actually be over-vaccinating and may be responsible for many of today's canine health problems.

Mindful of that, the current AAHA guidelines on vaccinations also strongly suggest that veterinarians and owners consider a dog's individual needs and exposure before they decide on a vaccine protocol. Many dog owners now do annual titer tests to check their dog's antibodies rather than automatically vaccinate for parvo or distemper.

Your vet will advise you exactly about timing, when your dog can be exercised in public places after the course is complete, and when boosters are due. Many vets now send reminder notices close contact with other dogs in the waiting room, nor indeed the waiting room floor!

Some people prefer not to subject their animals to routine vaccinations, but opt

Know your Beagle's ways so that you know when he's feeling blue or under the weather. If he's sleeping more than usual or is generally lethargic, have your vet check him out.

for boosters, but you should still make a note on your calendar for if over-due it will probably be necessary to give the full vaccination program again. If you are visiting your vet for an initial vaccination program, do not allow your dog to come into for a homeopathic alternative. This needs to be carried out to the letter, so you must ideally be guided by a vet who also practices homeopathy. Also bear in mind that it will probably be difficult to find a kennel that accepts a dog without proof of a routine vaccination program.

PREVENTIVE CARE
If your puppy has been bought from a truly dedicated breeder, all necessary care will have been provided, not only for the litter but also for the dam. She will have had regular health checks and boosters, with a worming routine. These will stand her puppies in good stead and provide them with greater

Dogs can pick up parasites, toxic chemicals and thorns and burs in the lawn. Check your Beagle over carefully after he's been sniffing around the yard.

immunity than would otherwise be the case.

It is also of great importance that any recommended tests for genetic abnormalities were carried out prior to the mating. A genuinely caring breeder will only have bred from a sound, healthy bitch and will have selected a stud dog of similar quality.

When your Beagle goes along to the vet for booster vaccinations, your vet will also give a brief routine health check-up. If the vet you use does not do this as a matter of course, request that the heart is checked while visiting, especially if your dog is past middle age.

NEUTERING/SPAYING
Whether or not you opt to have your dog spayed is a matter of personal choice, and some breeders strongly urge pet owners to do so. Discuss with your vet when is the appropriate time to have your dog neutered or your

A healthy pet Beagle, given the proper care, exercise and nutrition, will live to be a hearty 12 or 14 years of age.

bitch spayed. Never allow a vet to spay your bitch until after her first season. Timing "mid-season" will usually be advised.

Should you decide on neutering your male dog or spaying your bitch, you will have to take special care with subsequent weight control, though if the dog is exercised regularly this should be a problem. In some cases, an aggressive or over-dominant male can be easier to cope with after neutering, but this is by no means always so.

Veterinary research reveals that there are many positive health advantages to spaying/neutering, including the prevention of pyometra and uterine cancer in the bitch and testicular cancer in the dog. It also reduces the chances of prostate cancer in males, and in the case of a monorchid or a crypotorchid, your vet may well advise castration, as dogs with these hereditary conditions should never be bred.

YOUR BEAGLE AND HIS VET

Overview

- Select your veterinarian carefully. Consider location, cost, service, table-side manner and emergency clinic services when making your decision.
- Discuss the CORE and non-CORE vaccines with your veterinarian and establish an inoculation schedule for your puppy.
- Keep track of your Beagle's vaccinations, the date the injection is given, the dosage and the type.
- Preventive care saves hardship and hard cash. Invest in your dog's health so that you don't have to pay out for treatments, surgeries and medication in the future.
- Spaying and neutering offer many health advantages to pet dogs, including the prevention of cancers and pyometra.